This is the journal of

_____

The Breakthrough Series

Break Through to Freedom Journal

Discover the keys to healing, freedom, ⤙ and living God's promises ⤚

Kimberlyn McNutt

Most G.G. Publishing Company products are available at special quantity discounts for bulk purchase for sales promotions, premiums, fundraising, and educational needs. Inquiries for bulk orders or for speaking engagements email inquiries to info@journeyforfreedom.org.

Break Through to Freedom Journal
by Kimberlyn McNutt
Published by G.G. Publishing Company
290 Norwood Avenue, Suite 204
Deal, New Jersey 07723
www.ggpublishingcompany.com

ISBN: 978-1-7969-2071-0

While the author has made every effort to provide accurate Internet addresses at the time of publication, neither the publisher nor the author assumes any responsibility for errors or for changes that occur after publication.

19 20 21 22 23 — 9 8 7 6 5 4 3 2 1

Printed in the United States of America

I dedicate this book to my partner in breakthrough, my husband, Antoine McNutt, and our children Josiah, Hannah, John, and Heaven. In all of you, I have found everything I didn't realize I needed and the best of all I could have ever dreamed. You all complete my life's puzzle and are the foundation of everything beautiful, valuable, and important to me. You are my inspiration on earth for greater and bigger. You prompted my desire for breakthrough in every aspect of my life. I thank God that He saw greater for me than I saw for myself by giving me each of you.

Table of Contents

Acknowledgement

I would like to thank my mom, Mary Sherman, for your unwavering strength, dedication and commitment to me and my siblings. There were many days and nights where you could have given up raising four children alone, but you didn't. You stayed the course and gave the best you had. From you, I learned strength, dedication, hard work, and commitment. Thanks for your support of me professionally, as a mom and wife, and now in ministry.

Apostle John Eckhardt, Prophetess Wanda Eckhardt, and family, I thank you for your love and care for our family and the destiny God has in us. Thanks for being excellent leaders of faith, character, discipline, integrity, and apostolic might in ministry, never forsaking the former for the latter. God orchestrated it so that Antoine and I met each other and discovered Crusaders Ministries at the same time. We immediately agreed that Crusaders was where we were to join, start our marriage, and be trained in apostolic works. There we were introduced to deliverance and prophetic ministry and works of healing and miracles. That was in 2007, and so much revelation, wisdom, training, and activation has happened since then. Now we train teams, prophesy, heal, cast out demons, and have an overall solid foundation for the apostolic works we are called to. Great blessings and honor to you all.

Prophetess Michelle McClain-Walters, you met us in a

season when all we saw was pain, but you saw promise. Thanks for more than a decade of faithfulness in mentoring us. You sowed many prayers and prophetic words in public and private. You covered us when I felt like giving up. You pushed us apostolically and stood on the frontlines with us every step of the way and with every promotion, new endeavor, transition, challenge, and spiritual attack. Thanks for never letting go. Thanks for your selflessness. Thanks for never giving up. Thanks for your sacrifices. Thanks for always giving truth. Thanks for every seed sown. Thanks for being a defense. I honor you and Pastor Floyd Walters and look forward to witnessing the great harvest God is about to do in church ministry with you all in this season.

Regine Jean-Baptiste, I am grateful to you for a number of reasons, but I am forever most thankful and grateful for your work to take these writings and pull together this first book for me. You and your work are priceless. God sees every seed you have sown. He is the Father of lights and may He release an equal or greater portion of favor and glory to you for all you have sown into the lives of many great ones, through your curriculum writing, publishing, and apostolic giftings. May God release bright lights in this now season of your life.

To every supporter—whether in attendance at Journey for Freedom events, through donations, or with volunteer service—I send heartfelt thanks. Thanks for your support with every small and large group session, in person and online class, workshop, social media teaching, coaching session, and ministry night. I thank you from the bottom of my heart for your support. For any and every way you have supported, I say thank you!

Introduction

One of the worst things we can do is lie to ourselves about ourselves. When we do this, we operate in deception, where positive change is blocked, greatly hindered, or flawed. We end up trying to change everything and everyone around us because we are sure the issue lies with them. When we are in deception we are misguided. We direct our efforts towards changing the wrong areas of our lives, or changing the right areas in the wrong way. This is because our foundation is weak.

The truth is, we all are guilty of this. Every one of us has some measure of unrighteousness and deceit in our hearts and minds. As Romans 3:10 states, there is no one righteous (without Jesus Christ), not even one. Jeremiah 17:9 puts it this way: the heart is deceitful above all things and beyond cure. Therefore, we should all aim to pursue a life journey of breakthrough. A breakthrough life is needed to bring healing to our past, to set us free, to love, and to experience the promises of God in every area of our lives.

God desires that we live a life of breakthrough because it allows truth to flow into our hearts and minds through Jesus Christ. This aligns us with our call as Christians to follow Jesus, who makes known to us all truth, wisdom, and understanding as we seek Him. This breakthrough journal is designed to take you through a thirty-one-day journey of truth, wisdom, and revelation. It will help you to:

- Expose areas of deception and break through dysfunctional thinking in your heart and mind
- Be renewed and planted in the perfect and righteous truth of Christ
- Be perfectly positioned to reap the fullness of God's rich blessings on a regular basis in your life

As you break through every door of limitation, you will access the perfect peace, protection, and prosperity in God that you need to live a life of freedom and breakthrough as you pursue your destiny.

Each day's reading includes: a scripture, brief teaching, three breakthrough keys, and a reflection to guide you in journaling. Before you embark on your journey to breakthrough, here are a few points to help you successfully complete this journal and maximize your time:

1. Review the referenced scriptures in the freedom teachings to gain even deeper revelation into the day's topic.
2. Take the time to journal to capture your newfound wisdom, guidance, revelation and direction from God. The wisdom shared on each page is rich, however the revelations you receive from God as you journal are equally valuable.
3. Don't read ahead. Though the teachings are short, take this journey one day at a time. Be sure to ponder each breakthrough key. If needed, read each day's entries several times until you understand the breakthrough keys of the day. Seek wisdom from God when you need more insight.

Blessings to you. And now let the breakthrough journey begin!

Day 1
I am...

Forget the former things; do not dwell on the past. See, I am doing a new thing! Now it springs up; do you not perceive it? I am making a way in the wilderness and streams in the wasteland.

—Isaiah 43:18–19

God is the great Creator. There is never a minute or second that goes by when He isn't establishing, making, or remaking something new. His creative power works to make and remake our hearts, minds, and all the blessings He longs to give us. The amazing thing about God's power to create is that whether we are awake or asleep, He is still doing something new.

Whether we desire it or not, God is doing new things. Whether we believe in it or not, whether we choose to see it or not, God desires and still does great and powerful new things around us and in our daily lives. God's creative ability is limitless!

Breakthrough Keys

The keys to breaking through the door of the old and into the new are to:

1. **Open Your Eyes** – We must open our eyes by lifting our thoughts and minds off of ourselves, out of our situations, and placing them on God.

2. **Acknowledge God** – When we lift our eyes and place them on God, we can begin to acknowledge the new things that God desires to accomplish in our lives.

3. **Enjoy Your Life!** – God wants us to enjoy our lives. So, begin to anticipate the joy that God will bring into your life as you break through the issues of the past through this Break Through to Freedom Journal.

Reflection

What am I expecting God to make anew for me as I journey through these next thirty days? *(We must expect to perceive the new.)*

Day 2
A Breakthrough Diet

It is written, "Man shall not live by bread alone, but on every Word that proceeds out of the mouth of God."
—*Matthew 4:4*

At some point in our lives, we all find ourselves in seasons of depression, sadness, and/or hopelessness. When this occurs, pause and ask yourself some questions:

- What unhealthy behaviors and mind sets did I feed myself with in the season prior to?
- Did I feed restlessness with a diet of busyness?
- Did I feed loneliness with a diet of sex or toxic relationships?
- Did I feed rejection by chasing approval?
- Did I feed trauma with denial?

We don't just wake up depressed, sad, broken, or empty. Our current situations and states of mind are direct results of what we have fed ourselves in prior seasons. Matthew 4:4 reminds us that God has a new diet for us to feast upon to live a breakthrough life full of hope and peace.

Breakthrough Keys

The keys to a breakthrough diet that result in a life of freedom are to:

1. **Feed Yourself with the Word** – We should feed our minds with the Word of God every day.

2. **Seek God's Presence** – Our primary focus should be to spend time in God's presence, listening to His voice as we read our Bible. Sustainable peace and prosperity can only be found through the ongoing nourishing of our hearts and minds in the presence of God.

3. **Don't Wait. Start Today!** – Don't wait for a season of adversity to start feeding yourself with a diet of scripture and God's presence. Start now.

Reflection

What am I expecting God to make anew for me as I journey through these next thirty days? *(We must expect to perceive the new.)*

Day 3
Breakthrough Faith

You were taught, with regard to your former way of life, to put off your old self, which is being corrupted by its deceitful desires; to be made new in the attitude of your minds; and to put on the new self, created to be like God in true righteousness and holiness.

—Ephesians 4:22–24

God is a God of movement. He is not a God of stagnation, fear, regression, or bondage. He is constantly moving and orchestrating our life's journey to help us reach His designed destination that is filled with blessings. God is opening up blessings in our lives, which manifest among us by faith. We must shift, stretch, and grow our faith by managing the release of the old, to receive all of God's promised blessings. We may stagnate ourselves for years because of our refusal to release the comfort of old thoughts, mindsets, and patterns. However, we have to make a decision to release the old because breakthrough faith requires a renewal! We must embrace the mind of Christ, which leads to new thoughts, mindsets, and patterns. We can't blame life on everything and everyone else. It's time to move out of this old way of thinking and living. You are going to need faith to make it through the remaining days of this journal. So, it's time to embrace God's desire to see you advance from faith to faith and glory to glory.

Breakthrough Keys
The keys to enter the door of breakthrough faith are to:

1. **Say Goodbye to the Old** – We must allow God to move thoughts, people, relationships, and resources in or out of our lives so that we are positioned for success.

2. **Receive New Patterns** – Let go of old patterns and receive God's good, pleasing, and perfect will for us as we study our Bible. Romans 12:2 advises us to not conform to the pattern of this world, but to be transformed by the renewing of our minds.

3. **Meditate** – God wants us to spend time thinking about all of the blessings He has for us, so that our faith can increase. Philippians 4:8 reminds us that whatever is true, whatever is noble, whatever is right, whatever is pure, whatever is lovely, whatever is admirable—if anything is excellent or praiseworthy--we are to think about such things.

Reflection

What mindsets, thoughts, and patterns are hindering me from living a breakthrough life? *(Research and note some scriptures about your main point of hindrance that you can use to meditate on when this pattern arises in your life. For example, if your hindering mindset is poverty, do a web search for "scriptures against poverty in the Bible" or "scriptures for wealth in the Bible." Then write them down to meditate on in the future.)*

_____

_____

_____

_____

_____

_____

_____

_____

_____

_____

_____

_____

Day 4
Breaking Through Chaos

Make it your ambition to lead a quiet life: You should mind your own business and work with your hands, just as we told you, so that your daily life may win the respect of outsiders and so that you will not be dependent on anybody.
— *1 Thessalonians 4:11–12*

Drama and trauma are the twins of brokenness. They desire to bring chaos to our lives. When chaos is present it makes it impossible to live a quiet life, mind our business, and work to the best of our ability as God prescribes for us in today's scripture. When we are living lives filled with drama and trauma, we are not living God's best for our lives. The blessing is that God desires to set us free! He wants us free of drama and trauma through the truth of His Word. As we apply God's Word, we will see the fruit of chaos in our lives exchanged for the joy of peace.

Breakthrough Keys

The keys to breaking through chaos and into prosperous living are to:

1. **Make Freedom Your #1 Ambition** – We must make living a drama- and trauma-free life our number one desire. We must go after chaos-free living with everything we have.

2. **Mind Your Business** – Sometimes, when drama seeks to engage us in its storms, getting rid of chaos is as easy as minding our own business.

3. **Get Busy!** – The Living Bible translation of Proverbs 16:27 states that "idle hands are the devil's workshop." This is true. It's important to be in active pursuit of God's peace and His purpose for our lives.

Reflection

What are my ambitions? Do I believe God can help accomplish my goals? Where are drama and trauma inhibiting my abilities to establish goals? Where is drama and trauma inhibiting my progress towards achieving goals I've already established? How can I incorporate 1 Thessalonians 4:11-12 into my future plans and goals?

_____

_____

_____

_____

_____

_____

_____

_____

_____

_____

_____

_____

_____

Day 5
Breaking Through Pride

Humble yourselves, therefore, under God's mighty hand, that He may lift you up in due time. Cast all your anxiety on Him because He cares for you.

— *1 Peter 5:6–7*

Have you ever seen someone struggling and offered to help them, only to have them turn you down? Have you ever met someone so obsessed with themselves that it's as if they are sucking the air out of the room? How about the person who treats everyone like half of a human being to make themselves feel important? These are all manifestations of pride, which can look like independence, narcissism, vanity, arrogance, and conceit. Pride can also manifest itself in false humility, where we do not value ourselves according to God's identity for our us. We must be on guard for pride as we seek to live a breakthrough life, because it is one its biggest hindrances. Pride keeps us from showing vulnerability, where we act as if everything is fine, when all the while we are falling apart on the inside. God's desire is that we walk in humility through vulnerability. This draws us close to Him, so that we can be healed with His love. The more we receive His love, the more we are open to the help of others.

Breakthrough Keys

The keys to breaking through the door of pride and walking in a humility that brings freedom, healing, and abundance are:

1. **Showing Vulnerability** – Building a lasting relationship with God requires vulnerability and trust. Know that God can be trusted and wants you to share everything with Him so that you can receive healing and His perspective.

2. **Be Honest** – Humility takes honesty, so reveal your secrets to God and with those whom He leads you to share. This is when real healing and breakthrough occurs.

3. **Full Dependence** - Live a life where you are fully dependent on God and ask Him for people who model what healthy relationships looks like.

Reflection

What are my ambitions? Do I believe God can help accomplish my goals? Where are drama and trauma inhibiting my abilities to establish goals? Where is drama and trauma inhibiting my progress towards achieving goals I've already established? How can I incorporate 1 Thessalonians 4:11-12 into my future plans and goals?

_____

_____

_____

_____

_____

_____

_____

_____

_____

_____

_____

_____

_____

Day 6
Breaking Through Shame

You, dear children, are from God and have overcome them, because the one who is in you (God) is greater than the one who is in the world.

— 1 John 4:4

No one is exempt from experiencing shame. The key to overcoming shame is to be intentional about rejecting it. This means not entertaining it in your heart. Humiliation and distress caused by shame can leave us feeling embarrassed and full of guilt. It causes us to see ourselves in a lower place than what God intended for us. Yet, God wants us to know that the temptations, words, and situations that brought shame in our life are insignificant compared to the awesomeness of being His child. Regardless of how we feel, how we are treated, or how we have failed, as a believer in Jesus Christ we are always in the highest place of authority. In Christ, we are rulers in God's kingdom. God desires us to break through the door of shame. He desires for us to use the power He has given us over strongholds, temptations, gossip, or anything else that Satan tries to set against us. It's our season to break through shame and live in the abundant blessings of God's power and authority!

Breakthrough Keys

The keys to breaking through the door of shame into freedom are to:

1. **Release People, Situations, and Yourself** - You have to forgive yourself and others. Letting go of shame also requires releasing any guilt and condemnation from the associated people, situations, and yourself.

2. **Come Out of Agreement** - You must come out of agreement with every lie of the enemy that seeks to keep you in a place of shame. *(example: "You have gone too far", "God will never forgive this", etc.)*

3. **Receive God's Grace and Mercy** - The grace of God is sufficient. Starve every area of shame by choosing daily to live powerfully, and to stand by faith in the grace and mercies of God.

Reflection

How is shame keeping you from walking through the doors of God's promised freedom? What is the main thing that you need to eliminate to see shame leave your life?

_____

_____

_____

_____

_____

_____

_____

_____

_____

_____

_____

_____

_____

_____

Day 7
Breaking Through Anxiety

For the Spirit God gave us does not make us timid, but gives us power, love, and self-discipline.

— 2 Timothy 1:7

Anxiety is a destiny killer. It is the false and temporary perception of a fear or threat. And it keeps us hidden in a box called "what if." Anxiety comes not to just steal your destiny, but to literally cut off your breath. Anxiety has a variety of manifestations. It can often manifest dramatically with panic attacks or subtly in our inability to take risks, which kills faith. You must be determined to destroy the very anxiety seeking to kill you. When anxiety goes unchecked, it leads to anxious behavior. This results in decisions that are premature, irrational, and rooted in fear. Anxious thoughts and fear are not of God. They are sent by Satan to provoke us to move out of the will of God. Don't allow anxiety to cause you to move into what may feel like a real and never-ending nightmare.

Breakthrough Keys

The keys to breaking through the door of anxious thoughts are to:

1. **Focus on God's Love** – The love of God is a weapon of victory. When we are filled with God's love, we are able to face every anxious thought with victorious thinking!

2. **Tap into the Power of the Holy Spirit** – The Holy Spirit has the power to break us out of every limitation the enemy desires to place on us. Cultivate a deep relationship with the Holy Spirit to see His power over anxiety arise in your life.

3. **Practice Self-Discipline** – Breakthrough comes by being disciplined in pursuing the truth of God above all other choices. When anxiety wants to come, you must choose God's peace.

Reflection

What are some of my recurring anxious thoughts? God help me to identify the source of these anxious thoughts. *(Look through your Bible or do a web search to identify scriptures you can use to fight against anxious thinking.)*

_____

_____

_____

_____

_____

_____

_____

_____

_____

_____

_____

_____

_____

Day 8
Breaking Through Grief

Blessed are those who mourn, for they will be comforted.
— Matthew 5:4

Grief binds and will lead us into a grave place unless we process and heal from it. As you deal with loss, ask yourself: "Is a loss actually a loss if I grew and became a better and stronger person from that experience?" "Is a loss truly a loss if, from that process, I learned more about myself and my life's purpose?" "Did I indeed lose out if I stayed in character through the battle, in spite of all the negativity that was done to me?" We must examine places of grief in our lives and ask ourselves honest questions. If the individual we were in relationship with didn't value or love us enough to respect us and keep us around, then how much did we really lose? God desires to not only help us heal from grief, but also to help us learn and become a better person from our loss. We must be willing to let God partner with us to break through the door of grief, to healing and empowerment.

Breakthrough Keys

The keys to breaking through grief's door and walking in healing and freedom are to:

1. **Take Inventory** – Take the time to consider what you think you lost, versus the reality of that situation. Reality is truth and God is the best revealer of truth, so involve God in this process and be open to His response. To effectively take inventory from a place of reality you need to pray and ask God to: shine His light of truth into your situation, and help you to see, hear, and embrace the truth He releases.

2. **Ask God to Heal It** – Whether a perceived loss or actual loss, the pain and scars can be very real. Ask God to heal you and make you whole in each place of your heart where you have experienced feelings of loss.

3. **Receive the Better** – Ask God to use this grief for His glory! God can turn mourning into dancing by helping you to live a new, healthy, and joy-filled life after grief.

Reflection

What is my biggest source of grief? What is it about this particular loss that is causing me to mourn? What lessons have I learned from this time of grief? *(Ask God to heal your grief, and having faced it, to show you wisdom on how to proceed into your destined future.)*

_____

_____

_____

_____

_____

_____

_____

_____

_____

_____

_____

_____

_____

Day 9
Breaking Through Frustration

A person's wisdom yields patience; it is to one's glory to overlook an offense.

— Proverbs 19:11

We must be on guard for the subtle deception of frustration. It happens to us so quickly. One moment you are feeling discontented, disappointed, or defeated and before you know it you are angry, and living in aggravation. This is because frustration drives restlessness and anxiety, which cause ungratefulness. And that leads to rebellious behavior or depression. When we experience something that makes us upset or annoyed, and we don't take the time to deal with it, it will fester and grow. Frustration unchecked will cause you to ignore warning signs and to move full speed ahead out of the will of God. It can also cause you to overlook the great blessings already existing in your life, and to reject those who are closest to you. Everyone may experience frustration, but God's Word has the keys to help you break through the frustration into encouragement, joy, and His blessings.

Breakthrough Keys

The keys to breaking through the door of frustration are to:

1. **Stop!** – When offense, discontentment, or disappointment come our way, we need to stop and process it.

2. **Name It** – As you process the point of frustration, you can name it for what it is and honestly seek to receive God's healing. This prevents it from becoming toxic in your heart and mind.

3. **Take Your Feelings to God** – Ask God to help renew your mind with His Word and to renew your heart with His love for you.

Reflection

What past offenses have opened the door to frustration in my life? As I consider those past experiences what caused the frustration? God help me to identify the root of my frustration? Now that I know the root of this frustration, how can I be more intentional in the future to recognize when it is seeking to make its way back into my life?

_____

_____

_____

_____

_____

_____

_____

_____

_____

_____

_____

_____

_____

_____

Day 10
Breaking Through Insecurity

Then God said, "Let Us make man in Our image, in Our likeness..."

— Genesis 1:26

For You created my inmost being; you knit me together in my mother's womb. I praise you because I am fearfully and wonderfully made; your works are wonderful, I know that full well.

— Psalm 139:13–14

Insecurity seeks to attack us with lies and doubt. It is a feeling that causes us to think that we are inadequate, and it manifests in hesitation or disbelief. Insecurity can cause us to sabotage our own success while leading us to engage in actions that damage our relationships. We must be swift in dealing with insecurity, because we are fearfully and wonderfully made in God. He doesn't want us to be living in hesitation. He wants us to be certain of His love, power, and approval! God is ready to help us break through our insecurities and help us to embrace the confidence, conviction, and belief found in the truth of His Word.

Breakthrough Keys

For those who are ready to break through the doors of insecurity and into the assurance of your God given identity, the keys are to believe in:

1. **God's Image** – Fix your eyes on God's identity—who He is. You are made in His image and likeness. Get to know God and you will get to know yourself.

2. **Christ's Sacrifice** – Jesus's life, ministry, death, and resurrection give you the ability to be everything God says you are. You must believe in Christ and His gift of life for you.

3. **God's Vision** – Exchange your vision of yourself with God's vision for your life, circumstances, and identity through prayer and reading God's Word.

Reflection

Finish this prayer to God concerning your insecurities:

God, I thank You so much for the great thought You put into creating me. I have always been at the forefront of Your mind and heart since the beginning of time. You are the author of the universe, the creator of the heavens, the King of all nations and You loved me enough to create me in Your image and after Your likeness. Help me to...

_____

_____

_____

_____

_____

_____

_____

_____

_____

_____

_____

_____

Day 11

Breaking Through Fear of Man

Fear of man will prove to be a snare, but whoever trusts in the LORD is kept safe.

— Proverbs 29:25

We spend so much time worrying about what someone else can do or has done to impact our lives, our success, or our future. We can quickly become paralyzed with fear as we contemplate how others perceive us. When we are trapped in the opinions of others, we take our focus and reverence off of God and place it on an individual. However, the truth is, we have the greatest power to impact what happens in our own lives. We can choose to bow down to our fear of people, and thus, disobey God by not trusting Him. Or, we can break through our fear of others by surrendering every web of ambiguity, insecurity, and fear the enemy unleashes against us. God's powerful love for us has the ability to break through the fear of man and refocus our minds on the goodness of God.

Breakthrough Keys

The keys to breaking through every door the fear of man sets up against you are to:

1. **Focus on God** – We can focus on people or we can focus on God. Breakthrough starts with making a decision to focus our heart on God.

2. **Learn God's Love** – Understanding God's love casts out every fear we have in our lives. Spend time looking at Scripture to understand God's love for you.

3. **Trust God** – When we root ourselves in God's love it helps us to place our trust in Him -- not people.

Reflection
What steps can I take to begin believing and receiving God's love for me?

Day 12
Breaking Through Past Hurts

Create in me a pure heart, O God, and renew a steadfast spirit within me.

— *Psalm 51:10*

There is a saying, "closed mouths don't get fed." The same is true for closed hearts. Imagine your hand is your heart. Make a fist with your hand. Can anything be put in your hand now? When we keep our heart closed by tightly holding on to past hurts and pains, we are doing ourselves a disservice. We keep the healing and blessing of God from flowing in our lives. We may think we are protecting ourselves, but when we close our heart to people, we also close it to God. Breaking through past hurts is going to require you to open up your heart and let God in to help you release some things. When we are willing to open our hearts to God, then we can be fed from the healing bread of God that gives us joy, peace, and whatever else we need.

Breakthrough Keys

The keys to breaking through the doors of past hurts are to:

1. **Open Our Heart** - Healing past hurts takes opening our heart to let God and others in to help us.

2. **Forgive Yourself and Others** - We release the situations, circumstances, and individuals of the past by genuinely forgiving others, ourselves, and God.

3. **Receive God's Grace** - When we have opened our heart to God's grace and forgiven past hurts, we can receive true healing that brings joy, peace, and blessings.

Reflection

Is my heart open to God's healing power? What situations or individuals do I need to forgive, so that I can fully receive God's love?

_____

_____

_____

_____

_____

_____

_____

_____

_____

_____

_____

_____

_____

_____

Day 13
Breaking Through Unbelief

May the God of hope fill you with all joy and peace as you trust in him, so that you may overflow with hope by the power of the Holy Spirit.

— *Romans 15:13*

Self-help author, Napoleon Hill, is credited with saying, "Whatever the mind of a man can conceive and believe, it can achieve." This quote is accurate because life is first lived through our minds. Every victory you will ever experience first begins in your mind. Healing and prosperity begin in our minds. The enemy seeks to keep God's promises from manifesting in our lives through unbelief, which also begins in our minds. When we are operating in unbelief it robs us of peace, joy, and hope. It makes it hard for us to not only stand in God's truths, but also to see those truths when they are fulfilled in our lives. God wants us to break through the door of unbelief into the abundance of His promises.

Breakthrough Keys

We must rise up and fight against unbelief by deploying the keys of:

1. **Examining Your Mind** - All success begins in your mind, but failures start there as well. Examine all that comes through your mind.

2. **Fighting Unbelief** – You must fight unbelief by taking every negative thought captive and choose thoughts of success.

3. **Winning in Truth** – As you cast down negative thoughts of unbelief, you must replace them with the truths of God found in the Bible. This will help you win the fight to see God's promises manifest in your life.

Reflection

What is the biggest area in my life where I find that I have to fight to believe God? What are the thoughts of unbelief that arise in my mind concerning this area? Looking through Scripture, what are some winning truths *(versus)* that I can use to fight against thoughts of unbelief?

Day 14
Breaking Through Negative Mindsets

"For my thoughts are not your thoughts, neither are your ways my ways," declares the Lord. "As the heavens are higher than the earth, so are my ways higher than your ways and my thoughts than your thoughts."

— *Isaiah 55:8-9*

Negative mindsets come from ideas, thoughts, and attitudes that are birthed from experiences and modeled behavior by parents or guardians. These convictions create limitations in our hearts, which make us unable to see God's promises. For example, if you experienced poverty as a child your approach to money will stem from a poverty mindset. It can manifest in one of two ways: either you are always lacking, or you hoard and hold on to money so that you don't end up in poverty again. These negative mindsets must be healed because God desires for us to live in abundance. God's blessings can be delayed if He has to fight through mindsets of poverty, perversion, shame, or addictions. And once we do receive His blessings, we don't want them to be sabotaged. The good news is that God stands ready to help you break through every negative mindset.

Breakthrough Keys

You can have an optimistic mindset and see tangible blessings manifest in your life as you apply these keys of breakthrough:

1. **Submit to God** – We must submit every mindset to God. Whether those mindsets are generational, cultural, or created out of our own beliefs, we must exchange every attitude for God's truth.

2. **Remember God's Promises** – Come against wrong mindsets that seek to control your outlook in life by remembering the promises of God.

3. **Live God's Best** – Once you take the limitations off of your heart and mind and elevate your mind to Kingdom beliefs, enjoy the best God has to offer.

Reflection

What do I believe is God's best for my life? What mindsets are
hindering me from living in God's best for my life?

_____

_____

_____

_____

_____

_____

_____

_____

_____

_____

_____

_____

_____

_____

Day 15
Breaking Through the Middle

Let us not become weary in doing good, for at the proper time we will reap a harvest if we do not give up.
— *Galatians 6:9*

It's easy to trust God in the beginning of the journey, when your optimism, excitement, and energy levels are fresh. It can also be easy to trust God in the end when the finish line is in sight. However, the true testament of our faith lies in the in-between time. When you are in the middle of something that seems hard and requires a lot of work and time, does your heart profess that God is still faithful, or does it believe He has forgotten about you? Does your mind say that God's grace is sufficient so I'm going to trust in Him, or do you get frustrated and strategize ways to help God out because He is taking too long? A wise and successful warrior doesn't fight every battle; he or she only fights battles they will most likely win. These types of battles come with rewards that are worth the investment of time, strength, and energy. As you are now midway through your journey of diligently seeking breakthrough in your life, take some time to reflect on how far you have already come.

Breakthrough Keys

The keys to breaking through the temptation to stop in the middle are to:

1. **Remember the Good** – In the middle of any journey, we must remind ourselves of the good that God has already done in our lives and use that as inspiration to keep going.

2. **Examine the Bad** – Take the time to look at opportunities for growth so that you can implement changes to help you successfully make it to the finish line.

3. **Stand on God's Promises** – When all is said and done, breaking through the midway point takes standing on the promises of God. Remember what motivated you to start this journey and believe God to help bring you to completion.

Reflection

What am I most looking forward to as I continue my breakthrough journey? What am I least looking forward to on this journey? *(Write a prayer asking God to bless and assist with both of these expectations and hesitations moving forward.)*

_____

_____

_____

_____

_____

_____

_____

_____

_____

_____

_____

_____

_____

Day 16
Breaking Through Obstacles

"And we know that in all things God works for the good of those who love him, who have been called according to his purpose."

— *Romans 8:28*

Life is filled with obstacles. These can be simple hurdles like a closed road on a long commute, to mountain-like obstacles that can be a matter of life or death. Obstacles can delay our progress, bring us to a complete standstill, and even lead to anxiety, offense, or harm. The blessing in this is that God can use obstacles to open new doors of opportunity, life, and blessings for us. Obstacles don't have to lead to a dead-end road. They can be opportunities that lead you to great victory. This is why we can't get frustrated, sad, or depressed when obstacles arise. When we invite God to give us a fresh perspective concerning setbacks, temptations, or overwhelming obligations, He will empower us to see the opportunities that are before us. We'll be able to see where God's goodness and glory can manifest in our lives.

Breakthrough Keys

The keys to breaking through the door of every obstacle with a fresh outlook from God are:

1. **God is Good** – God is a Good Father who is always looking for ways to bring good fruit into the lives of His children. In the midst of obstacles remember God's character as good.

2. **Look for Good** – If you remember the truth about God's goodness, then you can remember to expect and look out for it no matter what obstacle stands before you.

3. **Do Good** – Don't let your life become an obstacle or a stumbling block for someone else. Always look for ways that you can demonstrate God's nature to others by doing good.

Reflection

Where have I seen God's goodness manifesting in my life?

_____

_____

_____

_____

_____

_____

_____

_____

_____

_____

_____

_____

_____

_____

_____

_____

Day 17
Breaking Out of Cycles

Ask and it will be given to you; seek and you will find; knock and the door will be opened to you. For everyone who asks receives; the one who seeks finds; and to the one who knocks, the door will be opened.

— *Matthew 7:7–8*

Cycles are born out of gaps in our hearts and minds, areas of brokenness, wrong desires, and faulty thinking. For example, if you see a cycle of perversion or sexual sin in your life, it's due to issues related to your identity. Cycles must be dealt with, or else they can affect everything in your life. Whatever has formed a gap in your heart or mind will eventually come out in your choices and decisions. It will even be evident in who you attract. So, when you find yourself in dysfunctional cycles that you can't seem to break, those are the moments when you must turn to God in prayer. We should constantly ask God to reveal gaps in our hearts and minds. We must seek God to give us the strength and wisdom to address all secret things and to uproot wrong desires and thoughts. We can seek breakthrough from bad cycles, knowing that God promises that everyone who asks will be given an answer, everyone who seeks finds, and to everyone who knocks, the door will be opened to them.

Breakthrough Keys

The keys to breaking through the door of bad cycles and living the fruitful, joyful, peaceful, and prosperous life God promises are to:

1. **Ask** – When you see brokenness begin to manifest in and around you, it's time to begin asking God in prayer to reveal the gaps in your heart and mind.

2. **Seek** – We must seek God's wisdom and strength through prayer to help us break cycles of dysfunction.

3. **Knock** – Continue to pray until you see every bad cycle—unhealthy relationships, destructive thinking, or harmful choices—stop in your life.

Reflection

What are some negative cycles that I have noticed in my life? Spend some time in prayer asking and seeking God to reveal the gaps in my heart or mind that allow these cycles to continue. *(Write a prayer that you can continually to use to "knock" in a place of prayer until you see these cycles cease in your life.)*

_____

_____

_____

_____

_____

_____

_____

_____

_____

_____

_____

_____

_____

Day 18
Breaking Through Weariness

Do you not know? Have you not heard? The Lord is the everlasting God, the Creator of the ends of the earth. He will not grow tired or weary, and his understanding no one can fathom. He gives strength to the weary and increases the power of the weak. Even youths grow tired and weary, and young men stumble and fall; but those who hope in the Lord will renew their strength. They will soar on wings like eagles; they will run and not grow weary, they will walk and not be faint.

— Isaiah 40:28–31

Feeling fatigued is a natural part of the human experience. This is because our bodies have limitations. These limitations are an opportunity to see God's great power at work within us as we rest. However, when we don't take the time to rest and be rejuvenated, we open ourselves to weariness. Weariness happens when we surpass a state of fatigue and become physically and mentally exhausted. It is a weapon the enemy uses against us to keep us from having the strength, encouragement, and empowerment we need to fulfill our purpose. God wants us to break through weariness so that we can receive the abundant, never-ending supply of strength and power found in His presence.

Breakthrough Keys

The keys to breaking through weariness are to:

1. **Tag God In** – When we are weak, God's grace, strength, and power are made strong in us. When you are feeling weary, tag God in by asking Him in prayer to help you.

2. **Rest** – Jesus says in John 15:5 resting in God causes us to bear fruit. If you want to see better fruit in your life, you need to rest in God.

3. **Start Again** – Once you have gotten rest, it is time to start again with new energy, ideas, and strength to continue your journey.

Reflection

Do I take intentional time during my day, week, month, and year to rest in God? What does intentional time of rest look like for me? What can I do today to begin taking the appropriate time to rest in God?

_____

_____

_____

_____

_____

_____

_____

_____

_____

_____

_____

_____

_____

Day 19
Breaking Through Death

The thief comes only to steal and kill and destroy; I have come that they may have life, and have it to the full.
— *John 10:10*

Anything that isn't growing is dying or dead. Being stagnant in fear or in disobedience to God brings death by killing our destiny. Continually tolerating identity issues, not seeking help for trauma, or making excuses for bad behavior is very costly. Death will manifest in our lives in the form of sickness, lost purpose and time, or the inability to finish tasks. This is not God's will for our lives. God desires for you to flourish, while Satan desires to come in like a thief to steal, kill, and destroy. God offers us abundant life, so that even if we make bad decisions, He can still help us to grow and thrive. Any area of your life that is dying, whether it be your health, career, education, relationship with God, finances, or family can be renewed. If you turn it over to God, He can breathe life upon it. God wants you to break through death by embracing the promise of an abundant life through Jesus Christ.

Breakthrough Keys

The keys to breaking through the door of death to life and purpose are to:

1. **Keep God's Promises in View** – It helps to know God's promises for abundant living in every area of our lives by reading the Word of God.

2. **Discern God's Promise** – When we know God's plans but are not seeing those plans manifest in our life, we can rise up and confront the plot of Satan to steal, kill, and destroy.

3. **Be Consistent** – We must be in constant communication with the Holy Spirit to ensure that we are living the abundant promises of God in every area of our lives. Seek to establish a way of living that consistently produces and progresses forward in a positive way.

Reflection

As I evaluate every area of my life such as health, career, education, relationship with God, finances, family, etc., am I growing in these areas? In which areas am I experiencing death? What is one thing that I can do to get back on track and experience God's full abundance for my life?

_____

_____

_____

_____

_____

_____

_____

_____

_____

_____

_____

_____

Day 20
Breaking Through Negative Self-Talk

The tongue has the power of life and death, and those who love it will eat its fruit.

— Proverbs 18:21

What were the conversations you had with yourself... like today? Were you even conscious of the thoughts running through your head? When the constant internal noise in our mind is negative— "I'm not doing enough", "I'm not good enough", or "Nobody likes me anyway"—we must pay attention to it. Negative self-talk impacts your confidence, joy, energy, strength, health, and effectiveness. People who are prosperous mentally, physically, spiritually, financially, relationally, and in other areas of life choose to be conscious of their thinking. They don't allow their minds to constantly wander into negativity. They also don't allow others to haphazardly speak into their lives. They are diligent about speaking positive words, affirmations, and decrees inwardly and outwardly. God desires for us to guard our words both internally and externally by speaking His blessings over our lives. We must become intentional about speaking the promises of God over our lives: daily, hourly, minute-by minute, and if necessary, second-by-second, until we see them manifest.

Breakthrough Keys

The keys to breaking through the door of negative self-talk are to:

1. **Pay Attention** – When negative self-talk is rising within you, out of your mouth, or from others, don't dismiss it. Pay attention!

2. **Correct Talk** – Monitor negative self-talk so you can correct it with the truth of God's promises.

3. **Be Your Biggest Cheerleader** – Cheer yourself on by declaring the promises of God over your life!

Reflection

What are some of the negative things I say to myself? *(Write down some positive affirmations you can consistently speak over your life to help you break through the door of negative self-talk.)*

_____

_____

_____

_____

_____

_____

_____

_____

_____

_____

_____

_____

_____

_____

Day 21
Breaking Through Limitations

*As the heavens are higher than the earth, so are my ways
higher than your ways and my thoughts than your thoughts.*
— *Isaiah 55:9*

What would it look like if we lived as if we truly believed God's power was limitless? If we were honest, most of us would admit we live like God can run out of blessings. This type of belief breeds faithlessness because we think God's blessings are finite and not always available for us. It can also manifest as jealousy. When we see others receive blessings we want, we become jealous and begin to view God's ability to bless as limited. However, we must break through every temptation to place limits on God. We must remember the blessings of God, for His people are as limitless as the heavens above, as numerous and full of power as the stars in the sky, and as countless as the grains of sand on the seashore. To see it, we simply need to stretch our faith!

Breakthrough Keys

The keys to breaking through every door of limitation are to:

1. **Recognize the Limits** – We must examine our hearts and minds and see where we have placed limitations on God's ability in our lives.

2. **Decree** – When we find places where we are limiting God, we must begin to declare or speak the truth of God against those limits.

3. **Believe** – Now, it's time to trust God to manifest His limitless power in your life.

Reflection

God please show me any limits I have in my heart and mind concerning your ability to provide for me, love me, protect me, and forgive me. *(Open your heart to God's power to remove those limitations by writing decrees that you can pray to remind you of God's limitless power.)*

_____

_____

_____

_____

_____

_____

_____

_____

_____

_____

_____

_____

_____

_____

Day 22

Breaking Through Double-Mindedness

But when you ask, you must believe and not doubt, because the one who doubts is like a wave of the sea, blown and tossed by the wind. That person should not expect to receive anything from the Lord. Such a person is double-minded and unstable in all they do.

— James 1:6–8

Double-mindedness causes us to not have a clear understanding of God's will and desires for our lives. In double-mindedness, our heart, will, and intellect cannot follow God's heart. This spins a web of anxiety, feelings of inadequacy, and destructive thoughts around us. That is why Scripture says a double-minded person is unstable in all his ways. The instability has the power to rule our lives through cycles of rejection and rebellion. Yet, God desires that we are stable and walking in wholeness. God has designed for us the keys to break through every form of instability that would seek to come into our lives. God's antidote to double-mindedness is to ground our lives in Christ, which gives us the power to live a well-balanced life. Through Jesus Christ, we also are able to access God's sufficient grace and great mercy. This can heal rejection in our lives, deal with past hurts, help us to forsake rebellion, and develop obedience to God out of love.

Breakthrough Keys

The keys to breaking through the door of double-mindedness, and walking in the acceptance and obedience of God are to:

1. **Acknowledge God's Faithfulness** – Double-mindedness is born out of the inconsistencies of others, experiences, and from ourselves. Acknowledging God's faithfulness and the fact that He never changes reminds us of the stability He desires for our lives.

2. **Seek Stability** – We must seek the stability that is available in Jesus Christ. We must remember that God will never fail us.

3. **Extend Grace and Mercy** – No one is perfect. If we want others to accept us and not get caught in a web of rejection and rebellion from hurts, we must be willing to extend grace and mercy to those around us.

Reflection

In what areas of my life do I feel like I am lacking a clear understanding of God's will and desires? *(Write a prayer asking God to help bring clarity to your heart and mind, so that you will not be double-minded when it comes to His faithfulness to His promises.)*

_____

_____

_____

_____

_____

_____

_____

_____

_____

_____

_____

_____

_____

_____

Day 23
Breaking into Clarity

If any of you lacks wisdom, you should ask God, who gives generously to all without finding fault, and it will be given you.

— James 1:5

There may be times in our lives when we have certainty about what we are called to be and do. Sometimes we think we have it all figured out. But after years of experiencing the unexpected and facing challenges, we might find our mindsets about our calling completely broken and stretched. This is usually uncomfortable, but it opens the door for God's true destiny to emerge in our lives. I believe this is what God desires for every single one of His children. God wants to move us from our own understanding to His revelation. He wants to partner with us to break through what we think we know, to what He has designed for our lives. Prayerfully, you have been experiencing this throughout this journal. God's desire is to continue to give you even more revelation concerning your heart, mind, and soul as well as your call and life's purpose. When we seek God's wisdom, we are able to break through uncertainty into the clarity of God for our lives.

Breakthrough Keys

The keys for breaking into clarity of our call and purpose are to:

1. **Inquire of God** – Whenever we lack clarity in anything, whether it be our call and purpose, or in smaller life matters, we can ask God through prayer to help us.

2. **Be Flexible** – Sometimes we have an idea in our minds and refuse to let it go. Our callings and purpose belong to God, so once we receive clarity from God, we must be willing to be flexible to incorporate His wisdom into our lives.

3. **Make Changes** – Don't be afraid of making the changes God is communicating to you about your calling and purpose. In the right timing, those changes have the power to help you fulfill your destiny for the glory of God.

Reflection

As I have worked through this journal, where have I seen God provide clarity concerning my purpose and calling. Have I ever inquired of God regarding my purpose and calling? Have I inquired recently? What is He saying?

_____

_____

_____

_____

_____

_____

_____

_____

_____

_____

_____

_____

_____

Day 24

Breaking into the Truth

Then you will know the truth, and the truth will set you free.

— John 8:32

Sometimes the best thing that you can do for yourself is to admit that you are broken, that you don't know, and that you need help. Those three simple words, "I need help," can save the lives of so many, but are rarely said. Often, people think that when they tell the truth they will be rejected or turned down. Others may feel like speaking honestly will be hard. But, speaking the truth was never meant to be that way. God wants us to share the reality of our lives with others— to testify—so that He can use our circumstances to reveal His truth to them. When we allow God's truth to be revealed in our lives it not only blesses us, but it also has the power to set others free. God wants to break us into truth, not truth as the world sees it, but truth through the lens of Jesus.

Breakthrough Keys

The keys to breaking into the door of truth that truly sets us free are to:

1. **Be Open** – Truth comes when we are open to receiving it in our lives and circumstances. We must open our hearts and minds to see, hear, and experience God's truth.

2. **Be Free** – Be free by being honest while on your journey for freedom. Know that God can take your reality and turn it into a testimony.

3. **Be Available** – Be available to allow God to use your testimony to bring healing to others.

Reflection

What do I believe is holding me back from seeking, living, and announcing God's truth? Why do I believe this is my particular barrier? What can I do about it?

_____

_____

_____

_____

_____

_____

_____

_____

_____

_____

_____

_____

_____

Day 25
Breaking into Right Expectation

Above all else, guard your heart, for everything you do flows from it.

— John 8:32

Finally, brothers and sisters, whatever is true, whatever is noble, whatever is right, whatever is pure, whatever is lovely, whatever is admirable—if anything is excellent or praiseworthy— think about such things.

— Philippians 4:8

What are your expectations for yourself, your family, schooling, or business? Are you in expectation of good or bad things to happen? Do you expect to experience support or sabotage, success or failure, or for people to pour in to your life versus taking away from it? Whatever we expect in life is what we tend to attract. This is because what we pay attention to the most and acknowledge in our life will manifest. If your expectations are negative, you will attract negativity since you are mostly paying attention to, and thinking or speaking about your negative life experiences. Breaking into right expectations requires you to stand guard over negative expectations in your heart and mind. We must break through the negative expectations and begin declaring, in faith, the positive promises of God, until we see them manifest in our lives.

Breakthrough Keys

The keys to breaking into right expectations and walking through the door of manifested promises are to:

1. **Stand on Guard** – Stand guard against meditating on your negative life experiences.

2. **Think Positively** – Focus on the positive things God is doing in your life. Store those positive memories in your heart and constantly replay them.

3. **Anticipate God's Promises** – Speak positively over all that is important to you and expect God to bring His promises to completion in your life.

Reflection

As I near the end of my breakthrough journey, how will I guard my heart and mind against negative thoughts, mindsets, and actions, so that I can set and embrace right expectations in God?

_____

_____

_____

_____

_____

_____

_____

_____

_____

_____

_____

_____

_____

_____

_____

Day 26

Breaking into Love

There is no fear in love. But perfect love drives out fear, because fear has to do with punishment. The one who fears is not made perfect in love. We love because He first loved us.

— 1 John 4:18–19

God is a God of overflowing love. He wants you to understand and to experience His love in every area of your life. He wants us to believe in love, hope in love, and trust in love again. Where we have been tainted from negative experiences with love and friendships, God can restore and heal us. Where we have the wrong understanding about love, God wants to renew our minds with His true love. God wants us to break into the door of His love, so that we can experience what He feels towards us at each moment of every day. We must engage God today to break up any and all blockages in our heart. These blockages prevent us from feeling and experiencing the love God has for us through Him and through others.

Breakthrough Keys

The keys to breaking into the doors of love that make us whole in every area of our lives are to:

1. **Remember Love** – We must remember that God's love is free and abundantly available to each and every one of us. This will help us to seek His love in every area of our lives.

2. **Experience Love** – God wants to demonstrate His love to us, and He wants our hearts to be open to experience His love through others.

3. **Give Love** – Once we have recognized and experienced God's love, we must pour it out on everyone we meet so that they will desire to know and love God as well.

Reflection

What has been my experience with God's love? What has been my experience with loving others? Is my heart open to love? Is my heart healed? Is my heart overflowing with love for others? Is my heart in need of healing from God? *(If love is lacking in any of these areas, ask God to heal these areas, and fill them with His love.)*

_____

_____

_____

_____

_____

_____

_____

_____

_____

_____

_____

_____

_____

Day 27

Breaking into Your Identity

But you are a chosen race, a royal priesthood, a dedicated nation, [God's] own purchased, special people, that you may set forth the wonderful deeds and display praises of Him who called you out of darkness into His wonderful light.

— 1 Peter 2:9

There are so many things that war against our identity. Our experiences from childhood, trauma, and even things in our environment like culture, media, arts, and entertainment, can impact our identity. The identity that we have formed from these influences must be examined through the lens of who we are in Jesus Christ. God does not want to limit our individuality, character, and personality, to the things we have seen in the world. God wants us to turn to Him, so that He can show us our own uniqueness that He designed for us before we were born. We should desire to break into God's identity for our lives and set our minds to press ahead with our eyes fixed on God. When we are not deterred or swayed by the identities of our family, experiences, and environment, then we are open to discovering our 'true' selves as God designed us to be.

Breakthrough Keys

The keys to breaking into the door of your true identity as a 'chosen people, a royal priesthood, a holy nation' are to:

1. **Assess Where You Stand** - Understand how your family, experiences, and environment have affected your identity.

2. **Put on the Robe** – Every day, we must put on God's identity in Jesus Christ, like a robe fit for royalty. After all, we are royalty in Jesus Christ!

3. **Walk It Out** – When your 'true' self is unfolding and being unveiled by God's Word, the best thing you can do is walk through the door of that truth by living it out every day!

Reflection

What aspects of my identity have I discovered as I have spent time journaling? What aspects of my identity would I like God to provide more clarity on? *(Ask God to provide that clarity now.)*

_____

_____

_____

_____

_____

_____

_____

_____

_____

_____

_____

_____

_____

_____

_____

_____

Day 28
Breaking into Victory

For the LORD your God is the one who goes with you to
fight for you against your enemies to give you victory.
— Deuteronomy 20:4

Breakthrough living in every area of your life means making a commitment to not live as a victim. The issues of the past want us to lay down and play the victim role, but God's identity for us is to be a victorious warrior. We are victorious not out of our own strength, but out of the victory that God won through the death and resurrection of Jesus Christ. Therefore, we must commit to making our life a no-victim zone, so we can soar into God's blessings for our lives. If something isn't going right or the way you want in your life, then it's your responsibility to be honest with yourself about the situation. Self-victimization accomplishes nothing. It is self-defeating and self-destructive and causes you to embrace powerlessness. God wants you to overcome today and take your place of victory through Jesus's blood on the cross.

Breakthrough Keys

We can break into the door of victory with the keys of:

1. **Know You're Greater** – No matter what you are facing, identify the true source of the issue and remind yourself that you are greater than it.

2. **Create a Plan of Action** – Once you identify the issue you need to face, seek God for strategies to victory.

3. **Adjust Accordingly** – Once you have a plan, be open to making adjustments as the Holy Spirit leads. Remember, small progress is always better than no progress.

Reflection

In which issue(s) that I am currently facing, do I want to see the complete victory of God? What are some strategies that I can use to see total and complete victory? *(Take some time to pray and see what strategies God gives you to use for victory.)*

Day 29

Breaking into Peace

Do not be anxious about anything, but in every situation, by prayer and petition, with thanksgiving, present your requests to God. And the peace of God, which transcends all understanding, will guard your hearts and your minds in Christ Jesus.

— Philippians 4:6–7

Do you know that you can be calm and not at peace? Someone can seem calm on the outside, but on the inside, their heart and mind are filled with conflict. That's because calm is an outward expression while peace is an inward truth. We cannot manufacture peace. God is the only One who can give us peace through Jesus Christ—the Prince of Peace. The blessing is that we don't have to live in anxiety, fear, or torment of past memories as we seek God's peace. We can ask God to send us the Spirit of Peace, which is the Holy Spirit, to bring us true peace in every area of our lives. When we have true peace in our hearts, it will reflect outwardly in many ways.

Breakthrough Keys

The keys to break through peace that settles every storm in our lives are to:

1. **Be Anxious for Nothing** – You have to make up in your mind that you will refuse to be worried about things that only God can fix.

2. **Pray** – Once you stop worrying, turn that energy toward God in prayer. Ask God to give you His peace.

3. **Show Gratitude** – Philippians 4:6–7 reminds us to live in gratitude. Being thankful changes our attitude and perspective and opens our hearts to God's peace.

Reflection

God, I ask you to reveal to me any areas of my life where I currently lack your peace. Show me where they are so that I can submit them to you. God, how can I maintain the peace that you have given me in this process as I prepare to complete this breakthrough journal?

_____

_____

_____

_____

_____

_____

_____

_____

_____

_____

_____

_____

_____

Day 30
Breaking into My Next Season

There is a time for everything, and a season for every activity under the heavens: a time to be born and a time to die, a time to plant and a time to uproot, a time to kill and a time to heal, a time to tear down and a time to build up, a time to weep and a time to laugh, a time to mourn and a time to dance, a time to scatter stones and a time to gather them, a time to embrace and a time to refrain from embracing, a time to search and a time to give up, a time to keep and a time to throw away, a time to tear and a time to mend, a time to be silent and a time to speak, a time to love and a time to hate, a time of war and a time of peace.

— Ecclesiastes 3:1–8

Times and seasons are a constant in life. Everyone has a time to be born and a time to die. During our time on earth, we experience seasons such as weeping, laughing, silence, and speaking. You can experience one moment of joy and grief in the next. We may not always have the opportunity to select what season we are experiencing, but we can decide how we live through these times and seasons. We can experience all the moments of life in our own power and strength, or we can invite God into our midst and rely on His strength. On the journey to breakthrough, we have to make a decision if we will ask God to be with us, or if we will leave Him waiting on the sidelines.

Breakthrough Keys

The keys to breaking through to your next season, beyond this time of journaling and examining your life are:

1. **Assess Your Time and Season** - Take an inventory of what season you are currently in. If you desire to change, now is the time to seek God.

2. **Choose to journey with God** - Breaking through the next season of your life will always require a decision to choose God.

3. **Pray for Grace** - Pray that God gives you grace, wisdom, and strength, to not only choose Him in this season, but in all future seasons.

Reflection

As I take a moment and evaluate my current time and season. What season and time do I believe I am in according to Ecclesiastes 3:1-8? What season and time do I believe God wants to usher me into next? Do I believe God was with me in this past season? How did I journey with or without God in this past season while I worked through this Break Through to Freedom Journal process? Did I choose God consistently on the journey? If no, what hindered me from making a choice to choose God? *(Seek God, write a prayer of mercy, and consider how those hindrances can be addressed moving forward for more of God.)*

_____

_____

_____

_____

_____

_____

_____

_____

_____

_____

Day 31
A Breakthrough Prayer

I will give thanks to you, LORD, with all my heart; I will tell of all your wonderful deeds.

— Psalm 9:1

Congratulations! You have put in the work and time to press through the doors of hindrance. Now you are on your way to living a breakthrough life where you are healed of the past, free to love, and continuing your journey into every promise God has for your life. Let's end our time in prayer:

God of the Breakthrough, I give You thanks for what You have accomplished within my heart, mind, soul, and body over this month. Lord, I ask that You continue to give me singleness of heart. Jesus, let Your thoughts be my thoughts, your words be my words and your voice be my voice. I whole heartedly invite you to continue transforming my mind.

Holy Spirit, I ask for the wisdom to know the important things. Let Your will for my life become my most important desire. Grant me grace so that the things in my heart that seem hard to obtain, maintain, and sustain would become easier as I partner with You. Because I decree You are the Author and Source of all we need, I commit to being in Your presence and being in tune with Your heart. Thank You for Your presence that will give us all we will ever need with joy and peace. We pray and decree these things in Jesus's name. Amen.

Reflection

Now that you have completed all thirty-one days of your Break Through to Freedom Journal, write down your plans for maintaining freedom.

_____

_____

_____

_____

_____

_____

_____

_____

_____

_____

_____

_____

_____

_____

_____

About the Author

Kimberlyn McNutt is a much sought-after freedom strategist and deliverance minister. She is well-respected and greatly honored for her keen ability to teach and minister deliverance in a manner that identifies and attacks the demonic roots of bondages for instant and long-lasting life transformation. Kimberlyn and her husband Antoine established and oversee the work of Journey for Freedom, an international deliverance work, that provides online and in-person courses, deliverance prayer ministry, and Freedom Nights focused on equipping individuals with the artillery needed to conquer various life challenges and entanglements of demonic bondage. Forged out of necessity and demand for a complete, peaceful, and discreet deliverance process, Kimberlyn and Antoine's ministry was launched when influential Christian leaders from around the nation flew to the couple's humble Chicago home to receive from their anointed ministry.

Kimberlyn carries a strong mantle of love and has spent hundreds of hours ministering and tackling soul issues of sin, trauma, and demonic bondage with people from various industries, ethnicities, leadership levels, and socioeconomic backgrounds. Kimberlyn is a consistent staple of service in the local church, having served in various leadership capacities with ministry directed toward singles, married couples, and those seeking prophetic, deliverance, and altar ministry. She also helps support and facilitate education, small group, and counseling initiatives.

In addition to her extensive dedication to ministry leadership, in her professional career, Kimberlyn served in various director and manager positions within a multibillion-dollar school district, overseeing district-wide strategic improvement initiatives and programs. She also consulted for two Big Four public accounting firms and a Fortune 100 bank. Kimberlyn received her bachelor of science from the University of Illinois in Urbana-Champaign in finance with a concentration in accounting, and a master's in organizational behavior and change management from Benedictine University in Lisle, Illinois.

Kimberlyn McNutt is the wife of Antoine McNutt and together they greatly enjoy their first ministry of parenting their four children. For more information about Kimberlyn, please visit her website: www.JourneyForFreedom.org and follow her ministry on Facebook: www.Facebook.com/JourneyForFreedom.org (written and video testimonials and ratings included).